LONELINESS

RESOURCES FOR BIBLICAL LIVING

Lou Priolo, series editor

LONELINESS

CONNECTING WITH GOD
AND OTHERS

LOU PRIOLO

P&R PUBLISHING
P.O. BOX 817 • PHILLIPSBURG • NEW JERSEY 08865-0817

Unless otherwise indicated, Scripture quotations are from the ESV® Bible (The Holy Bible, English Standard Version®), copyright © 2001 by Crossway, a publishing ministry of Good News Publishers. Used by permission. All rights reserved.

Scripture quotations marked (NASB) are from the New American Standard Bible®. ©Copyright The Lockman Foundation 1960, 1962, 1963, 1968, 1971, 1972, 1973, 1975, 1977. Used by permission.

Scripture quotations marked (NASB95) are from the New American Standard Bible® (NASB), Copyright © 1960, 1962, 1963, 1968, 1971, 1972, 1973, 1975, 1977, 1995 by The Lockman Foundation. Used by permission. www.Lockman.org.

The Scripture quotation marked (NIV) is taken from the Holy Bible, New International Version®, NIV®. Copyright © 1973, 1978, 1984, 2011 by Biblica, Inc.™ Used by permission of Zondervan. All rights reserved worldwide. www.zondervan.com. The "NIV" and "New International Version" are trademarks registered in the United States Patent and Trademark Office by Biblica, Inc.™

Scripture quotations marked (NKJV) are taken from the New King James Version®. Copyright © 1982 by Thomas Nelson. Used by permission. All rights reserved.

Italics within Scripture quotations indicate emphasis added.

Portions of this booklet have been adapted from Lou Priolo, "Why Are You Lonesome Tonight?," chap. 7 in *Picking Up the Pieces: Recovering from Broken Relationships* (Phillipsburg, NJ: P&R Publishing, 2012), 51–55.

ISBN: 978-1-62995-920-7 (pbk)
ISBN: 978-1-62995-926-9 (ePub)

Printed in the United States of America

Library of Congress Cataloging-in-Publication Data has been applied for.

OVER MY many years as a biblical counselor, at least half of all my shepherding ministry has been devoted to marriage counseling. But when I moved to Atlanta to serve as the director of counseling at Christ Covenant Church, the demographic of my counseling load changed significantly. The most amazing thing about this, from my perspective, is that I will turn sixty-eight years old later this year, yet the young people of the congregation (mostly between the ages of twenty-three and thirty-five and many of them single) are coming to an old guy like me for answers to life's problems. I am a very blessed man! God has been and is very good to me.

My new position, which I took on around the beginning of the COVID pandemic, opened my eyes anew to a growing problem in our culture. Although I have written briefly about the subject of loneliness before,[1] it has become necessary for me to delve deeper into the Scriptures to address this issue in a more robust manner.

What you read in this volume may offer you sufficient help all by itself. I pray that is the case. But the booklet is also intended to be used in the context of biblical counseling. Its various checklists and worksheets will enable a trained pastor or biblical counselor to not only help you get to the bottom of your loneliness but also facilitate your spiritual growth as you learn to apply the Scriptures to your life. The Spirit works through the Word! I trust that you, and the saints at Christ Covenant, will find help and hope in the pages that follow.

---

1. See Lou Priolo, "Why Are You Lonesome Tonight?," chap. 7 in *Picking Up the Pieces: Recovering from Broken Relationships* (Phillipsburg, NJ: P&R Publishing, 2012).

It's an Epidemic!

Loneliness has become a worldwide epidemic.[2] It can be excruciatingly painful. What's more, it can be deadly. Research now indicates that persistent loneliness (loneliness that lasts for more than two weeks) may be deadlier than alcohol abuse, obesity, and cigarette smoking. Lonely individuals may be at greater risk of stroke, coronary artery disease, high blood pressure, anxiety (perhaps most notably, pessimism about their future), depression, poor cognitive performance, cognitive decline, post-traumatic stress syndrome, and dementia.[3] They also are prone to be reckless. The intense pain and sadness they experience often impel them to try to tranquilize themselves by drinking excessively, cutting themselves, using illegal drugs, or practicing sexual promiscuity.

If you are reading this booklet, you are probably more familiar with the symptoms and miseries of loneliness than you want to be. But there may be a few details you have not yet considered. In the inventory below, I have assembled some of them in the hopes that you will be able to better understand the extent to which you may be experiencing loneliness.[4]

Before you proceed, let me give you a word of hope. This booklet was designed not primarily to diagnose loneliness in the lives of Christians but to help to remedy it. So, regardless of what the inventory may reveal about your degree of loneliness, remember that there will be concrete, practical, biblical help and hope in the pages that follow.

2. In January 2018, the United Kingdom created an official office called the Minister of Loneliness.

3. It is believed that loneliness and social isolation negatively impact the body by increasing stress hormones and inflammation and interrupting healthy sleep patterns. This in turn compromises the immune system. A summary of the research is available in Jed Magen, "This Is Why Loneliness Is Bad for Your Health," World Economic Forum, February 27, 2018, https://www.weforum.org/agenda/2018/02/loneliness-is-bad-for-your-health/.

4. This is not a scientifically normed instrument. It has been compiled largely from available research articles.

Here then is a little inventory that may help you to identify some of the possible precondition issues or component elements of your loneliness.

Loneliness Inventory

☐ I wish I had more and deeper friendships.

☐ I wish people would call or visit me more often than they do.

☐ I wonder who will help me or take care of me if I get into trouble.

☐ I wish I had someone to bounce my ideas off.

☐ I think I am unlovable (or a "loser").

☐ I wish I had more people with whom I could share my happy moments.

☐ It seems nobody really understands me—no one appreciates who I really am.

☐ I don't have anyone I can really trust.

☐ It seems that nobody needs me or wants to be with me.

☐ I find myself struggling with intense feelings of loneliness even when I'm in a room full of people.

☐ When I do make efforts to connect with others, my offers are not reciprocated.

☐ I have thoughts and feelings of worthlessness.

☐ I binge shop, snack, or stream (movies or TV shows).

☐ I'm tempted to tranquilize my sad feelings by turning to temporal things rather than things of eternal significance.

☐ I crave physical affection.

☐ I crave physical warmth (blankets, hot baths, and beverages).

☐ I allow my feelings of hopelessness and depression to keep me from regular personal Bible study and prayer.

☐ I give in to self-pity.

☐ I spend more than two hours each day on social media (other than for business purposes).[5]

5. Research indicates that people who spend more than two hours daily on social media are lonelier than people who spend only half an hour. See Brian A. Primack et al., "Social Media Use and Perceived Social Isolation Among Young Adults in the

□ I enter unhealthy relationships, or stay in them, out of fear of being alone.

□ I find myself increasingly participating in irresponsible or reckless activities.

□ I spend too much time by myself.

□ I find it difficult to find and make new friends.

Please keep in mind that even though you may be experiencing some of the above symptoms, we have not conclusively proved the cause is loneliness. A sore throat may be indicative of a cold, the flu, or something much worse. We will address some of the issues from the inventory in the following pages. But our goal is not primarily to eliminate the indicators but to treat the infection, whatever or wherever it may be.

You Are in Good Company

Can you think of anyone in Scripture who struggled with loneliness?

"I've never really thought that much about it. But I do know that no temptation can *overtake me* but that which is common to man. Other than maybe Naomi in the book of Ruth, and the prophet Jeremiah, I can't recall too many."

These are good examples. Naomi was bereft of her husband and two sons.[6] And Jeremiah, the weeping prophet, was told by God not to marry, and his life increasingly became more difficult.

Here are three more biblical examples.

Elijah said, "I have been very jealous for the LORD, the God of hosts. For the people of Israel have forsaken your covenant, thrown down your altars, and killed your prophets with the

---

U.S.," *American Journal of Preventative Medicine* 53, no. 1 (July 2017): 1–8, https://doi .org/10.1016/j.amepre.2017.01.010.
6. However, the Lord provided Naomi with Ruth, who was apparently better to her than seven sons.

sword, and I, even I only, am left, and they seek my life, to take it away" (1 Kings 19:10).[7]

King David was also well acquainted with loneliness: "Look to the right and see: there is none who takes notice of me; no refuge remains to me; no one cares for my soul" (Ps. 142:4).

The *apostle Paul* was abandoned by one of his closest friends and left alone.[8] He wrote to Timothy,

> Do your best to come to me soon. For Demas, in love with this present world, has deserted me and gone to Thessalonica. Crescens has gone to Galatia, Titus to Dalmatia. Luke alone is with me. Get Mark and bring him with you, for he is very useful to me for ministry. (2 Tim. 4:9–11)

In one of the most fascinating accounts in the New Testament, God opened up a door of ministry for Paul, yet he didn't go through it. Why? Some believe it may have been loneliness that caused him to take a different path:

> When I came to Troas to preach the gospel of Christ, even though a door was opened for me in the Lord, my spirit was not at rest *because I did not find my brother* Titus there. So I took leave of them and went on to Macedonia. (2 Cor. 2:12–13)

Loneliness is a common experience. It can be complex. It has many causes. It may or may not be the result of sin, but it can tempt one into sin—or further sin. God's grace is sufficient to help Christians to deal with each aspect of loneliness—its sources, its symptoms, its seductions, and its sting.

7. As it turned out, Elijah was not as alone as he—in his exhausted, undernourished, suicidal state of self-pity—thought he was (vv. 4–7). God told him, "I will leave seven thousand in Israel, all the knees that have not bowed to Baal, and every mouth that has not kissed him" (v. 18). And in his mercy, the Lord also gave Elijah a companion, Elisha (vv. 19–21).

8. I don't know about you, but every time I read the latter part of the book of Acts, I ask myself, "Where are all the other apostles in one of Paul's greatest times of need? Did no one from Jerusalem care enough to help and defend him? They certainly knew he was in trouble."

What Is Loneliness?

So, what exactly is loneliness? Is it the same thing as being alone? Many view loneliness simply as not having the company of others to enjoy. But loneliness is a compound emotion that not every person experiences exactly alike. For most, it involves sadness and feelings of isolation. For many, it involves shame, grief, anger, and a sense of inadequacy or inferiority. For some, it includes feelings of rejection, jealousy, and envy.

Is loneliness a medical disease?[9] Is it a genetic predisposition? Is it a sin? Is it an effect of circumstances? Or may we more broadly and accurately define it as a condition that is "common to man"? We will look at loneliness through several descriptive lenses over the course of this book, but our first and foremost lens is this: for the Christian, loneliness may be the result of a defective relationship with God.

Loneliness may also be the result of not being in or enjoying fellowship with God at all. Sometimes people are lonely because they have never been saved from their sin—they have never truly put their trust in Christ. Consequently, they have not been indwelt by the Holy Spirit and do not have his abiding presence in their lives.

Without Christ and his substitutionary death on the cross, we would be *alienated* from God: "Remember that you were at that time separated from Christ, alienated from the commonwealth of Israel and strangers to the covenants of promise, having no hope and without God in the world" (Eph. 2:12). Talk about being alone! When we put our trust in Jesus, however, he comes to indwell us—to keep us company, if you please. Jesus said, "If anyone loves me, he will keep my word, and my Father

9. Don't be surprised if loneliness begins to be viewed as some kind of mental disorder. If that occurs, look for pharmaceutical companies to invest lots of money to develop medications that will treat the symptoms of the new loneliness disorder. They'll likely not be able to treat the cause because fundamentally the cause is not organic.

will love him, and we will come to him and make our home with him" (John 14:23). Of course, once God is at home in us, he will do a whole lot more than keep us company!

As well as God the Father and God the Son, believers have one more companion to help them in their loneliness—one whom those outside Christ do not have. God the Holy Spirit is a real, living person—and a unique one at that! Do you perceive and appreciate and relate to him that way? After all, he has a personality. He has cognition and volition and relates to us through various affections. He is omniscient, omnipresent, and omnipotent. If you are a Christian, he dwells within you.

He is present to comfort and assist you, to intercede for you, to guide you, to convict you, to teach and enlighten you, to sanctify you, and to empower you. He is your constant companion. He is the source of your power and personal relationship to Jesus Christ. You can enjoy continuous fellowship with him if you want it. Having a right relationship with him is your key to living life in a manner that is both pleasing to God and satisfying to you.

Now, when I speak of your having "fellowship" with the Holy Spirit, I'm referring primarily to the assurance that comes from confessing and forsaking all known sin and the sense of closeness to God that comes from having a clean conscience and drawing near to him through Bible study and prayer. Such fellowship doesn't necessarily displace a person's desire for marriage or companionship, but it provides a sense of contentment that should blunt the edge of loneliness: "Let your conduct be without covetousness; be content with such things as you have. For He Himself has said, 'I will never leave you nor forsake you'" (Heb. 13:5 NKJV). I will say more about this later on.

Rethinking Loneliness

What would you say if I told you that you are going to have to repent of your loneliness?

"I'd say I'm not going to read another page of your booklet!"

Please stay with me a moment longer. It's not what you think.

The Greek word for *repent* fundamentally means "to rethink." I would like for you to *rethink* how you interpret loneliness. I would like you to view loneliness more through the lens of Scripture than through the lens of those who do not have an eternal perspective, as we do.

You see, in order to change your feelings, you have to change your thoughts as well as your actions. So, I would like to suggest (as have others) that loneliness starts as a state of mind before it becomes a feeling. The way you *think* about being alone affects the way you *feel* about it. If, for example, you believe that to avoid being lonely you must always have another human being at your side, you are likely to be a very lonely person indeed.

Although we may experience the complexities of loneliness differently, most of us think of it primarily as a very painful, debilitating emotion. Loneliness is indeed an emotion, but it is an emotion that God created—and, like every other human feeling, it serves a good purpose in our lives. Like a shrieking smoke detector or an annoying hazard light flickering on a car's dashboard, our painful emotions often function as indicators that we need to examine something in our lives more carefully—something is not as it should be, and there may be danger ahead. We could say that loneliness is God's smoke detector that lets us know it is time to draw closer to him.

For most of us, there are times, even in rooms filled with people, when we feel lonely. Yet if you arm yourself with the biblical mindset that loneliness is primarily the result of not enjoying communion with God, you may find that you feel less lonely even when you are alone. Consider these words of Jesus:

Indeed the hour is coming, yes, has now come, that you will be scattered, each to his own, and will leave Me alone. And yet I am not alone, because the Father is with Me. These things I have spoken to you, that in Me you may have peace. In the world you will have tribulation; but be of good cheer, I have overcome the world. (John 16:32–33 NKJV)

Jesus knew he was going to be forsaken by his disciples (John 16:32), but he also knew he wasn't really alone because the Father was with him. He viewed being *left alone* and being *lonely* as two different things. His mindset was not "I will necessarily be lonely as a result of being left alone" but rather seems to have been "As long as the Father is with me, I will not be lonely even though all forsake me." Jesus knew that God's presence and provision were more than adequate to make up for the loss of all other company.

Loneliness is sometimes the result of expecting others to meet our needs and coveting their attention and care rather than letting God sustain us. When loneliness results from such unbiblical thinking, it reveals an idolatrous heart.[10] While it is not wrong to experience human companionship, especially in the bond of matrimony, it is wrong to substitute human companions for God and place your faith in them instead of him. Have you ever been guilty of displacing God with some other person? Could loneliness be God's way of letting you know you have been guilty of idolatry?

"Well, maybe to some extent—but how can God, who is a Spirit, meet my desire for companionship?"

God is able to minister to us in our loneliness *through other people* and certainly does so at times. But he also ministers to us in a more immediate, direct, and personal way: *through prayer and the Word.*

A friend once told a story about a family of three whose car broke down late one night during a severe thunderstorm. It stalled right in front of an old farmhouse. The father ran up to the door of the house and asked the farmer if he would be willing to put his family up for the night. The farmer agreed to let them stay but explained that the extra bedroom contained only a set of bunk beds. The man thanked the farmer and quickly brought his wife and daughter into the house.

10. The Bible equates covetousness with idolatry in Ephesians 5:5 and Colossians 3:5.

As they settled into bed, the little girl was given the top bunk; the man and his wife took the bottom one. When the lights were turned off, the thunder and lightning grew worse. The little girl became frightened and asked her father for some comfort.

"Daddy, I'm afraid!"

"Now honey, there is nothing to be afraid of. . . . Jesus is up there with you," came the voice from below.

After a few moments, as the storm continued to rage, the little girl tried again.

"Daddy, I'm afraid!"

"Sweetheart, I told you there is nothing to worry about. The Lord is with you up there."

Suddenly a clap of thunder exploded very close to the farmhouse. The little girl cried out, "Daddy, can you please come up here with God and let me come down there with Mommy?"

For some, the thought of God comforting them in their loneliness is about as appealing as sleeping alone on the top bunk. "Thanks for the offer, but I'd rather be ministered to by someone with flesh and blood."

The Holy Spirit will comfort us in our loneliness as he will comfort us in any other trouble (2 Cor. 1:3–5). But he will do so in proportion to the time we spend in Bible study (in reading, memorizing, and meditating on Scripture) and prayer. The Spirit works in conjunction with the Word. You must provide the Spirit with his most powerful instrument if you want him to assist you in your trials.[11] Take up "the sword of the Spirit, which is the word of God" (Eph. 6:17 NASB), so that he will have what he needs to comfort you most effectively.[12]

If you are single and lonely, let me ask you how much time you would spend in the company of a boyfriend or girlfriend to cultivate a relationship. Five hours a week? Twelve hours?

11. God's Word, which the Holy Spirit himself has authored, is the means through which he works both directly and indirectly.

12. The word used for "word" here is *rahma*: the spoken word. The Spirit can most effectively use the Word when it is on the tip of your tongue, an indication that Scripture is already in your heart and thus ready to be used at a moment's notice.

How does the time you would like to spend with this person compare with the time you now spend in prayer and the Word? What do you suppose would happen to your loneliness if you spent even half as much time with God as you would with this person? What if you invested half as much time meditating on Scripture as you do longing for and imagining how wonderful it would be to have such a person in your life?

If you are lonely while married or in a relationship you hope will lead to marriage, let me ask you the same basic questions. How does the time you spend in the presence of your companion compare with the time you spend in prayer and the Word? What do you suppose would happen to your loneliness if you spent thirty percent of the time you spend with that person with God instead? What if you invested as much time meditating on Scripture as you do with your special someone? One final question is this: To what extent are you looking to that person to meet your needs and fulfill your desires instead of turning to God? (To what extent is your emotional umbilical cord connected more to that person than to God?)

"I hear what you are saying, and I can't disagree in principle, but practically speaking I need more than that. I mean, sometimes I just need a hug!!"

I understand. I really do. And your desire for companionship, and even hugs, is certainly not wrong in and of itself. But first things first. If you look *first* to other people rather than Christ's abiding presence and resources to deal with or tranquilize the pain of your loneliness, you will be disappointed—if not very frustrated. If you look to these people instead of to Christ, or more than you look to him, it's a clear indication that your desire to *not be lonely* is an idolatrous one.[13]

I just got off the phone with someone who inquired what I was doing today. When I explained that I was writing a booklet on loneliness, she asked, "Are you going to address the fact

---

13. To be free of loneliness is not a wrong desire per se, but it becomes idolatrous when we seek companionship on *our* terms rather than God's.

that some people have lots of friends but are lonely—they still long to have deep companionship with someone?" Even married people sometimes experience loneliness. So, a Christian's foundation for the solution to loneliness is first and foremost a willingness to cultivate intimacy with Christ through prayer and the Word. From this platform, other biblical solutions may be launched.

What Factors Contribute to or Cause Loneliness?[14]

A good number of things can cause or contribute to feelings of loneliness. As you read the following list, check each factor that you believe might be contributing to your loneliness. After you have finished the booklet, you may want to consider showing this inventory to your pastor, elder, or biblical counselor. Perhaps he or she can help you to identify the most significant contributing causes of or influences on your loneliness and can assist you with fleshing out the biblical remedies suggested in the latter part of the booklet.

☐ *You haven't been introduced to your Best Friend. (The Holy Spirit does not abide with you because you have not put your trust in Christ.)*

When we put our trust in Christ,[15] he sends his Holy Spirit to indwell us. The Holy Spirit is a real person, who, in a very real sense, becomes our closest companion.

14. Some of the material that follows has been adapted from the recording *How to Handle Loneliness* by Wayne Mack (available at https://noutheticmedia.com/shop /wayne-mack/mp3-audio-wm/how-to-handle-loneliness-mp3/). I also would like to strongly recommend chapter 6 of his book *Out of the Blues: Dealing with the Blues of Depression and Loneliness* (Bemidji, MN: Focus Publishing, 2006).

15. Meaning we are willing to turn away from our self-oriented way of living and to believe that Jesus the Son of God died as our substitute to take the punishment we deserve and to credit to our account his perfect righteousness.

You, however, are not in the flesh but in the Spirit, if in fact the Spirit of God dwells in you. Anyone who does not have the Spirit of Christ does not belong to him. (Rom. 8:9)

And because you are sons, God has sent the Spirit of his Son into our hearts, crying, "Abba! Father!" (Gal. 4:6)

Remember that you were at that time separated from Christ, alienated from the commonwealth of Israel and strangers to the covenants of promise, having no hope and without God in the world. (Eph. 2:12)

☐ *Your relationship with God has been interrupted, impaired, impeded, or otherwise inhibited.*

He who has My commandments and keeps them is the one who loves Me; and he who loves Me will be loved by My Father, and I will love him and will disclose Myself to him. . . . If anyone loves Me, he will keep My word; and My Father will love him, and We will come to him and make Our abode with him. (John 14:21, 23 NASB95)

Sometimes Christians are lonely because they do not cultivate an intimate relationship with Christ through prayer and the Word. It has been said that the essence of loneliness is being unaware of the One who is with us everywhere.

More than that, I count all things to be loss in view of the surpassing value of knowing Christ Jesus my Lord, for whom I have suffered the loss of all things, and count them but rubbish so that I may gain Christ, and may be found in Him, not having a righteousness of my own derived from the Law, but that which is through faith in Christ, the righteousness which comes from God on the basis of faith, that I may know Him and the power of His resurrection and the fellowship of His sufferings, being conformed to His death. (Phil. 3:8–10 NASB95)

Draw near to God and He will draw near to you. Cleanse your hands, you sinners; and purify your hearts, you double-minded. (James 4:8 NASB95)

☐ *You are living an isolated lifestyle.*

Sometimes we are isolated from others due to circumstances beyond our control. But sometimes we refuse to pursue relationships with other Christians out of pride ("I will not chase after them; they should seek out my friendship"), selfishness, or fear.

> Whoever isolates himself seeks his own desire;
> he breaks out against all sound judgment. (Prov. 18:1)

☐ *Your relationships with those close to you have been broken by illness, death, divorce, or some other isolating event or series of events.*

There are many things that God providentially brings into the lives of his children that cause us to be separated from our loved ones. Job is one example of someone who loved God but experienced unimaginable loss, including the deaths of all his sons and daughters (Job 1:13–19). To make matters worse, his wife and three of his closest friends increased his agony and sense of isolation by giving unbiblical advice. Like Job, we can become isolated through suffering and upheaval in our lives, especially when those around us do not offer godly support.

☐ *You are married, but your spouse does not love or communicate with you as he or she should.*

God designed marriage in part because most people would be lonely without a lifelong companion with whom they can share not only their physical possessions but also their hearts (Gen. 2:18–24). Sometimes in marriage, for one reason or another, this companionship is hindered. Perhaps your spouse is not a believer, is unwilling to communicate, or is unaware of the dynamics of biblical communication. This can be an especially painful kind of loneliness. Unbelieving spouses are simply not capable of communicating on a deep spiritual level because they do not have the Spirit.

> But a natural man does not accept the things of the Spirit of God, for they are foolishness to him; and he cannot understand them, because they are spiritually appraised. (1 Cor. 2:14 NASB95)

☐ *You are unmarried and are experiencing intimacy issues in a romantic relationship.*

Sometimes unmarried Christians who are in dating relationships find that they are lonely. There can be various causes for this,[16] but typically a lack of intimacy is at the heart of it. This may stem from a deficiency of intimate communication or from one party's unwillingness or inability to reveal his or her heart to the other person.

☐ *You have a diminished desire or ability to befriend others, perhaps due to a fear of intimacy.*

Christians are to be pursuers. We are to pursue love and the upbuilding of one another (Rom. 14:19), to pursue peace (Heb. 12:14), and to pursue those who are sinning and straying from the faith (Matt. 18:15; Luke 15:3–7; James 5:20). Sometimes we are hindered from pursuing others for a good reason, such as being physically unable due to illness or injury. Often, however, we allow pride and the fear of feeling awkward to keep us from interacting with those God wants us to love. "There is no fear

---

16. I have written a small book that may provide insight into some of the other reasons for this intimacy deficiency: *Danger Signs of an Unhealthy Dating Relationship* (Sand Springs, OK: Grace and Truth Books, 2016).

in love; but perfect love casts out fear" (1 John 4:18 NASB95).[17] When we give in to those sins, we end up practicing selfishness rather than demonstrating biblical love for God and neighbor.

☐ *You have a strong fear of being rejected—an insecurity that keeps you from getting close to others.*

Fear of being rejected often keeps us from loving and interacting with others. Rather than focusing on how we might love or minister to them, we focus on how they might hurt or reject us. We should be able to tell ourselves, "It doesn't much matter if I get rejected—being rejected is not a sin. What really matters is that I don't sin by failing to love my neighbor[18] with the same fervor and intensity with which I love myself." But more often we think, "I just couldn't bear it if one more person rejected me."

☐ *You are experiencing a transient lifestyle.*

In the United States, 25 percent of the population relocates annually. As a result of recent COVID-19 restrictions, many people around the globe have realized that their work responsibilities can be effectively accomplished outside their local offices, making mobility more possible than ever before. Even if you never leave your town or city of birth, family and friends may move away.

> Now it came about in the days when the judges governed, that there was a famine in the land. And a certain man of Bethlehem in Judah went to sojourn in the land of Moab with his wife and his two sons. The name of the man was Elimelech, and the name of his wife, Naomi; and the names of his two sons were Mahlon and Chilion, Ephrathites of Bethlehem in Judah. Now they entered the land of Moab and remained there. (Ruth 1:1–2 NASB95)

17. For much more on this topic, see my booklet *Fear: Breaking Its Grip* (Phillipsburg, NJ: P&R Publishing, 2009).

18. And who is your neighbor? Basically, your neighbor is any person God sends across your path. Check out Luke 10:25–37.

For some, this disconnection from home, especially from family and friends, contributes greatly to their sense of isolation and loneliness. This is just one reason why finding a solid church family in a new location *before* moving should be a matter of prayer and research. Making plans without considering God's priorities is unwise.

> Come now, you who say, "Today or tomorrow we will go to such and such a city, and spend a year there and engage in business and make a profit." Yet you do not know what your life will be like tomorrow. You are just a vapor that appears for a little while and then vanishes away. Instead, you ought to say, "If the Lord wills, we will live and also do this or that." (James 4:13–15 NASB95)

☐ *You have been spending an inordinate amount of time on social media.*

It has become increasingly easy to substitute real relationships with pseudo or surrogate ones. Rather than having true face-to-face fellowship with others and showing them genuine hospitality, it is easier to interact with people virtually.[19] As connected as we can be through the internet, social media is no substitute for live human interaction. It is very difficult, and in some cases impossible, to obey Scripture[20] without being geographically in the same place with other believers.

I have known people who have become so accustomed to virtual communication that they have grown uncomfortable with being in the physical presence of others, if not afraid. They

---

19. The word *fellowship* in the Bible is often found in the context of food and drink. Obviously, it is impossible to share a meal together virtually.

20. For example, those passages that encourage and require us to "meet together" (Heb. 10:25), show hospitality (Acts 2:42, 46; 20:7; Rom. 12:13; Heb. 13:16; 1 Peter 4:9), "greet one another with a holy kiss" (2 Cor. 13:12), participate in the Lord's table (1 Cor. 11:20–32), fulfill the Great Commission to baptize and make disciples (Matt. 28:19–20), fulfill several of the "one another" commands of Scripture (Rom. 15:7; Gal. 5:13; 6:2; Eph. 5:19), and, for that matter, be properly shepherded (1 Peter 5:2—note the phrase "the flock of God *among* you" in the NASB).

gradually lose touch with their families and friends and "forget" how to interact with them in a live social setting. Over time, such people increasingly struggle to reorient themselves to actual (in-person) interaction with others.

☐ *You are experiencing reproach for the sake of Christ or suffering for righteousness as a result of fulfilling your biblical responsibilities.*

As Christians, we sometimes acquire enemies because of the truth of the gospel (John 15:18; 1 John 3:1). Even if we don't make enemies, we may encounter others who censure and ostracize us.[21]

> If the world hates you, you know that it has hated Me before it hated you. If you were of the world, the world would love its own; but because you are not of the world, but I chose you out of the world, because of this the world hates you. Remember the word that I said to you, "A slave is not greater than his master." If they persecuted Me, they will also persecute you; if they kept My word, they will keep yours also. (John 15:18–20 NASB95)

> Blessed are you when men hate you, and ostracize you, and insult you, and scorn your name as evil, for the sake of the Son of Man. Be glad in that day and leap for joy, for behold, your reward is great in heaven. For in the same way their fathers used to treat the prophets. (Luke 6:22–23 NASB95)

When the prophet Elijah was hated and ostracized, he mistakenly thought he was all alone and wanted the Lord to take him home.

> Then he came there to a cave and lodged there; and behold, the word of the LORD came to him, and He said to him, "What are

---

21. I'm pretty sure that, back when I was single, I lost at least one woman I really wanted to date because someone gave her misinformation about nouthetic counselors. Then I met my wife, who was a Jay Adam's zealot, and the rest is history, as they say.

you doing here, Elijah?" He said, "I have been very zealous for the LORD, the God of hosts; for the sons of Israel have forsaken Your covenant, torn down Your altars and killed Your prophets with the sword. And *I alone am left*; and they seek my life, to take it away." (1 Kings 19:9–10 NASB95)

☐ *You are struggling with self-image issues.*

When we lack Christ-centered self-confidence, it is easy for us to assume that others are not interested in being our friends or even spending time with us.[22] This sense of being "unlovable" not only increases our awareness of being alone but often prevents us from reaching out to others or even participating in social activities. By contrast, the apostle Paul had a sense of certainty about what God was doing in his life and ministry: "I consider myself not in the least inferior to the most eminent apostles" (2 Cor. 11:5 NASB95).

☐ *You have patterns of unbiblical thoughts, motives, or attitudes that are off-putting to others and consequently contribute to or exacerbate your loneliness.*

I have saved this one for last for a good reason. In my years of counseling Christians, I have found this to be one of the most common sources or partial causes for their loneliness. At some level, it is probably true for most of us. Our thought patterns and motives are so unbiblical that they cannot be concealed. They make their way out of our hearts and manifest themselves in our words, attitudes, and actions. This, in turn, tempts others to want to avoid us. The solution is not to avoid people out of fear of being rejected but rather to allow the Lord to sanctify our thoughts and motives through the Spirit and the Word.

22. This lack of confidence is often due to the fact that we judge ourselves to be inferior in any number of areas. Those judgments may be accurate or inaccurate based on biblical values or cultural values. To learn more about how to maintain a biblically based self-image, please see my booklet *Self-Image: How to Overcome Inferiority Judgments* (Phillipsburg, NJ: P&R Publishing, 2007).

I will address many of the sins that lead to this more fully in the latter part of this booklet, but here is a checklist to get you started. Put a check next to the traits that you believe may be causing others to resist close friendship with you.

- ☐ Selfishness
- ☐ Pride
- ☐ Fear
- ☐ Worry
- ☐ Self-pity
- ☐ Suspiciousness
- ☐ Jealousy
- ☐ Irritability (sinful anger)
- ☐ Bitterness (resentment)
- ☐ Believing the worst rather than the best about others
- ☐ Other _____
- ☐ Other _____
- ☐ Other _____

What Are the Cures for Loneliness?

In addition to the primary cure—cultivating a relationship with Christ through prayer and the Word—here are some other useful, biblically based remedies to consider.[23]

1. Learn to view loneliness more as a blessing than as a curse.

Trials are unavoidable in this life. They are designed by God for your good. Loneliness is a trial, and a bit of loneliness is inevitable. Not all loneliness can be avoided—especially when it is not the result of our own sin. To expect to live a life in this

23. What follow are biblical means intended for those who are in Christ: his followers. They will not ultimately be effective for those who are outside Christ. If you have not recognized your need of his forgiveness or expressed a willingness to repent of your sins, your first step is to obey the gospel: to repent and turn to him in faith, believing that when he died, he paid the eternal penalty for all your sins.

fallen world without any loneliness is to magnify the miseries of your loneliness.

> Consider it all joy, my brethren, when you encounter various trials, knowing that the testing of your faith produces endurance. (James 1:2–3 NASB95)

As a Christian, you can learn to live with a little bit of loneliness. You can do—you can learn to do—all things through him who strengthens you (Phil. 4:13). And, if your loneliness is the result of your refusal to compromise your faith—for instance, by marrying an unbeliever or being in relationships with people who will cause you to sin—you are suffering for righteousness's sake and will be rewarded greatly in heaven.

2. Learn to take advantage of the benefits of a little loneliness.

Loneliness can be beneficial when it motivates you to do the following:

- to pray (Ps. 31; 142:2)
- to meditate on Scripture (Ps. 119)
- to examine yourself (Lam. 3:40)
- to think about one day being with Christ and all his saints in heaven, where you will be free of all loneliness (Rev. 21:2–4)[24]
- to be more aware of your need for others (1 Cor. 12:22–27)
- to know Christ more intimately (Phil. 3:10)

Loneliness can also be beneficial when it better equips you to minister compassionately to others (2 Cor. 1:3–5).

I can remember a time in my early twenties when I very much wanted to be married. There was one passage in Scripture

---

24. "We will never experience perfect or enduring fellowship with anyone in this world. But in heaven, where there will be no more sin and death, there will be no more broken relationships." Mack, *Out of the Blues*, 104.

that helped me through those difficult days—especially after I committed it to memory. Take a few moments to read this passage and consider its message to you.

"The Lord is my portion," says my soul,
 "therefore I will hope in him."

The Lord is good to those who wait for him,
 to the soul who seeks him.
It is good that one should wait quietly
 for the salvation of the Lord.
It is good for a man that he bear
 the yoke in his youth.

Let him sit alone in silence
 when it is laid on him;
let him put his mouth in the dust—
 there may yet be hope;
let him give his cheek to the one who strikes,
 and let him be filled with insults.

For the Lord will not
 cast off forever,
but, though he cause grief, he will have compassion
 according to the abundance of his steadfast love;
for he does not afflict from his heart
 or grieve the children of men.

To crush underfoot
 all the prisoners of the earth,
to deny a man justice
 in the presence of the Most High,
to subvert a man in his lawsuit,
 the Lord does not approve.

Who has spoken and it came to pass,
 unless the Lord has commanded it?
Is it not from the mouth of the Most High

that good and bad come?
Why should a living man complain,
 a man, about the punishment of his sins?

Let us test and examine our ways,
 and return to the LORD! (Lam. 3:24–40)

Here are some takeaways from the first two verses of this passage. They show how our souls are blessed when we use our loneliness as an opportunity to deepen our relationship with the Lord.

- "The LORD is my portion" (v. 24). The Lord will provide everything you need to be content.
- "Says my soul" (v. 24). You need to talk to yourself[25] rather than listen to yourself when you are lonely.
- "Therefore I will hope in him" (v. 24). In moments of loneliness, you ought to look to God before you look anywhere else.
- "The LORD is good to those who wait for him" (v. 25). If you expect to see the goodness of the Lord, you will patiently endure your trial.
- "The LORD is good . . . to the soul who seeks him" (v. 25). If you expect to see the goodness of the Lord, you will spend much of your alone time seeking him in prayer and the Word.

3. Evaluate your schedule in light of biblical priorities and be willing to remove or reprioritize certain activities.

I daresay that for some of you this may be both the most important and most difficult remedy for the problem of loneliness. But to effectively deal with your loneliness, you must be willing to rearrange your priorities. It's just that simple!

25. That is, you must remind yourself of the truth of Scripture rather than allow yourself to listen to the devil's lies.

Whether you are single or married, young or old, your ultimate priority is your walk with Christ. Everything else follows and flows from that. (Check out the list of responsibilities in Ephesians 5:18–6:9 and Colossians 3:16–4:1 to see what's at the top.)

The fact is, when our loneliness brings us pain, it seems easier to turn to temporal pleasures to tranquilize us or distract us from our pain instead of turning to God and pursuing the other remedies described in this booklet. If you are lonely, consider how much time each week you are spending in front of screens (smartphones, televisions, and computers). Below are some self-examination questions and spaces to record your answers.

- Exactly how much time each week do I seek pleasure in front of some kind of screen? _____
- How much of this time is an attempt to distract myself from my sadness or to tranquilize sad feelings? _____
- How much of this screen time shall I reclaim each week and instead devote to fellowship with God (and his people) through the biblical means of grace?
  - ☐ Fellowshipping with other Christians _____
  - ☐ Reading and studying God's Word _____
  - ☐ Praying _____
  - ☐ Meditating on and memorizing Scripture _____
  - ☐ Reading Christian books _____
  - ☐ Listening to or watching Christian sermons or podcasts _____
  - ☐ Ministering to or being ministered to by other believers _____

Are there any other superfluous pleasurable activities that you need to delete from or downgrade in your weekly schedules?

Activity	Reclaimed Time per Week
☐ Hobbies	_____
☐ Social media	_____
☐ Social events	_____
☐ Activities with friends that result in guilt rather than mutual edification	_____
☐ Unnecessary school activities or work done for the purpose of sinful people pleasing	_____
☐ Texting or phone calls	_____
☐ Other _____	_____

4. Become vitally involved in a local church that preaches and practices the Bible.

There is no such thing as a perfect church. But there are healthy churches that attempt to glorify God and minister to the needs of their members. God wants his saints to be united to local church bodies. The local church is one of God's means of grace—it is a resource through which God pours out his grace to his children. If you don't believe and apply anything else from this book, at least believe this: *it is not good for you to be disconnected!* You were born again to become a part of Christ's body, the church.

To forsake or dismiss active involvement in the body of Christ is to forsake and dismiss one of the three greatest sources of help in the universe.[26] What is mightier than they are to help you to grow spiritually and be conformed to the image of Christ? What can bring about more stability and lasting happiness than they?

26. The other two, which we have already discussed, are the Spirit and the Word of God.

And let us consider how to stir up one another to love and good works, not neglecting to meet together, as is the habit of some, but encouraging one another, and all the more as you see the Day drawing near. (Heb. 10:24–25)

How can a healthy local church help you with your loneliness?

- It can help you to grow in your walk with Christ. This will help to take the bite out of your sense of being alone.
- It can afford you with opportunities to fellowship with others in the church. This will cut out more of your alone time and provide you with any number of family members with whom you may share your life.
- It can provide you with individual friends.
- It can provide accountability to help you to overcome struggles with sin that, if left unchecked, will only increase your loneliness.
- It can provide you with opportunities to minister to and serve others. This will help you to focus on how you can love others more than on how others may not be loving you.
- The church can remind you of, and even personify, God's nearness.

5. Be willing to allow God to choose your friends.

Let me ask you a rather personal question: How do you choose your friends? Do you have a set of special criteria to determine who are "worthy" to be chosen as your friends, or are you willing to allow God to choose your friends based not on what they can do for you but rather on how you might be able to minister to them?

Now, I'm not suggesting that you lower your standards below what the Bible says is safe. In other words, I'm not asking you to violate Proverbs 13:20 (NASB95): "He who walks with wise men will be wise, *but the companion of fools will suffer harm.*" But I'm asking you if you have raised the standard for who qualifies as "friend worthy" higher than the standard of Scripture. Jesus was a friend to sinners (Matt. 11:19 and Luke 7:37–39). Are you willing to be?

If you have raised your standard for potential friends above the standard that Jesus requires, not only may you be guilty of showing partiality (James 2:9), but you also may be cutting off someone whom God intends to use to take the edge off your loneliness. Not only is this elitist attitude contrary to Scripture, hurtful to others, and a communicable sin (one that is easily transmitted to other people), it is the main reason some people are friendless and lonely.

For as long as I can remember, I have had two categories of friends.

- *Category A Friends.* These are friends whom I pursue primarily on the basis of how I might be able to minister to them. I know I may receive little or nothing as a result of my befriending them. These friends are plentiful and easily accessible.
- *Category B Friends.* These are friends that I pursue because I would like them to minister to me as well. In other words, I hope to be their friend on the basis of how we could minister to each other. These friends have been harder to come by and typically need to be sought out carefully with wisdom and much prayer.

The neat thing is that most of my current category B friends started as category A friends. Over time, they matured in their walk with Christ to the point where they are able to minister to me as effectively as I can minister to them—if not more so! Many have become my lifetime friends.

6. Identify and put off those sinful thoughts, motives, attitudes, and actions that are contributing to your loneliness (Eph. 4:22).

Certain sinful thoughts and attitudes fuel your loneliness and the misery that goes along with it. And other sins actually repel potential friends in one way or another. Of course, some transgressions of God's law fall under both of these categories. Sooner or later, if you do not deal with your mental-attitude sins, they will fester and metastasize to such an extent that they become obvious, surface sins.[27]

Anxiety (worry). Some people constantly worry about the future. They set their minds on every possible thing that could go wrong tonight, tomorrow, next week, next month, and even ten years from now.

- "It will be so awkward if . . ."
- "I couldn't bear the rejection if . . ."
- "What if I never find someone and end up being lonely for the rest of my life?"

Focusing on what might go wrong with your life in the future rather than on what God wants you to do with your life in the present[28] compounds the misery of your loneliness. Looking at life through the lens of worry is like projecting your worry on the wall of the future so that it appears much larger than it actually is.[29]

27. The truth is, this booklet would need to be six times longer to fully address all these sins. For now, all I am able to do is to help you to identify them and point you to some resources that have already been produced to help Christians to address each one.

28. "Do not be anxious about tomorrow, for tomorrow will be anxious for itself. Sufficient for the day is its own trouble" (Matt. 6:34).

29. There are many good biblically based resources available to help you to understand and correct worry. Among my favorites are Lou Priolo, "Dealing with Anxiety" (sermon, Valleydale Church, Birmingham, AL, March 31, 2019), https://www.competenttocounsel.org/how-to-deal-with-anxiety/; Elyse Fitzpatrick, *Overcoming Fear, Worry, and Anxiety: Becoming a Woman of Faith and Confidence* (Eugene, OR: Harvest House Publishers, 2001); and John MacArthur, *Anxious for Nothing: God's Cure for the Cares of Your Soul* (Colorado Springs: David C Cook, 2012).

Anxiety rarely shows up in a person's life alone. Sooner or later it invites its kinfolk: rash judgments, self-pity, jealousy, and suspicion.

Rash judgments. Once our thinking becomes distorted by anxiety, it's usually not long before we become prone to making judgments about people that are uncharitable and based on little or no evidence. Rather than believing the best about people as 1 Corinthians 13:7 requires,[30] we are quick to assume the worst—especially about their motives.[31]

Self-pity. At some point, if left unchecked, anxiety can lead us to question God's goodness, which can in turn lead us to become bitter toward him. Just like Job, we tell ourselves "It's not fair" or "God isn't doing what he's supposed to do." The next thing we know (if we even realize it at all), we feel sorry for ourselves and begin asking, "What's the use in trying?" Then we sulk and pout and murmur and complain against God.[32]

This victim mentality not only is evidence of an unthankful heart but also is usually rooted in doctrinal error. For example, you may think that God cannot be sovereign since he did not prevent something painful from happening to you—or that, if he is sovereign, he cannot be good. Self-pity is really a form of discontent that causes us to focus on what God hasn't given us more, or rather, than on what he has.

When the sin of self-pity tempts us to murmur and complain to God and to others, at some point (especially when this becomes a pattern) those around us become repulsed. This further intensifies our sense of isolation and our loneliness.

---

30. First Corinthians 13:7 teaches us that love "believes all things." This means that in the absence of evidence to the contrary, we should try to put the best interpretation on what other Christians do.

31. I've written a booklet about the various forms of this all-too-common problem and how to address it biblically: see *Judgments: Rash or Righteous* (Phillipsburg, NJ: P&R Publishing, 2009).

32. "When a man's folly brings his way to ruin, his heart rages against the LORD" (Prov. 19:3).

Put yourself in Moses's place for a moment. Try to imagine how he felt about being the target of Israel's self-pitying murmurs and complaints.

> Then they said to Moses, "Is it because there were no graves in Egypt that you have taken us away to die in the wilderness? Why have you dealt with us in this way, bringing us out of Egypt? Is this not the word that we spoke to you in Egypt, saying, 'Leave us alone that we may serve the Egyptians'? For it would have been better for us to serve the Egyptians than to die in the wilderness." (Ex. 14:11–12 NASB95)

Suspicion. People who worry are also prone to become suspicious of others. Lonely people often give in to the temptation to isolate themselves, which in turn can foster an untrusting attitude toward others—a tendency to believe the worst about others' motives rather than believing the best about them.

- "He doesn't really care about me."
- "She doesn't want to be my friend now. Maybe she never was."
- "The reason they never return my calls is because they think I'm pestering them too much."
- "True friends would check on me more often."
- "The people in my church are cliquish and hypocritical."
- "I just know they love to talk about me behind my back."
- "They constantly make excuses for not wanting to hang out with me."

While these statements are, sadly, sometimes true, suspicious people—rather than believing the best about even their friends—tend to believe the worst about others on very flimsy "evidence."[33]

33. One of the best remedies for these kinds of suspicious thoughts is to memorize Ecclesiastes 7:21–22: "Do not take to heart all the things that people say, lest you hear your servant cursing you. Your heart knows that many times you yourself have cursed

Covetousness, jealousy, and envy. Covetousness is wanting to have that which belongs to someone else. Envy is not only wanting to have it but also being upset or angry that the other person has it and you don't. The essence of jealousy is the fear that you are going to be displaced by someone or something else.

There is, of course, a selfless kind of jealousy.[34] But the self-focused fear that we might be replaced by another is unloving. Rather than rejoicing with a loved one at the thought that he or she is benefiting from gaining another good friend (Rom. 12:15), we selfishly focus on what we may lose if such a friendship develops. Sinful jealousy intensifies our loneliness as we imagine being even more isolated tomorrow than we are today.

Bitterness and resentment. Bitterness typically results when we do not biblically process the hurt we experience when others sin against us. It has been said that bitterness is like drinking poison and expecting your offender to suffer the consequences. It doesn't work that way. Bitterness is a condition that intrudes upon every area of our lives—especially our friendships. At first it may be undetectable by others, but in time it will manifest itself in dozens of ways: hypersensitivity, impatience, condescension, withdrawal, outbursts of anger, sarcasm, and more.[35]

Pride. Some people are lonely because they build walls instead of bridges. Let's do an experiment. Right here, right now, I would like you to think of the proudest person you know. Then ask yourself, "How excited am I about the prospect of getting closer to this person than I already am?" My guess is that no matter how

others." Suspicious thoughts are so common a problem among Christians that I have written a booklet to address it: *Suspicion: How to Overcome "Paranoid" Thinking* (The Woodlands, TX: Kress Biblical Resources, 2018).

34. God is a jealous God (Ex. 20:5). In 2 Corinthians 11:2–3, Paul demonstrates righteous jealousy.

35. To date, the best-selling title in the Resources for Biblical Living series is my booklet *Bitterness: The Root That Pollutes* (Phillipsburg, NJ: P&R Publishing, 2008). May I suggest you consider reading it if you suspect you have not forgiven someone in your life.

much you care for this person, their pride tempts you to hesitate to draw closer to them. There is something off-putting about proud people. Perhaps it is because we know that our ability to develop more intimacy with them will be greatly hindered by their unwillingness to acknowledge their own faults and failures.[36]

There are hundreds of ways pride can manifest itself in our lives and trip us up. But perhaps the most common way that pride traps us in our loneliness in particular is by making us not want to appear needy. At the end of the day, this has to do with our image in the eyes of others—our reputation. Lonely people sometimes do not reach out to those who love them and confess how miserable they are or how hard it is for them to be alone. They do not seek help because they believe it will mar their reputation.[37]

Repeatedly in the Scriptures we read and see that "God resists the proud, but gives grace to the humble" (James 4:6 NKJV; see also Ps. 138:6; Prov. 3:34; 29:23; Matt. 23:12; Luke 1:52; 1 Peter 5:5). The meaning of the word *grace* that is in view in these passages is not primarily "unmerited favor" but rather "help." God's help (his supernatural power that enables us to live the Christian life) is available to those who are willing to humble themselves. It requires a certain amount of humility to reach out to others when you are hurting and to let them know how much pain you are really in. Of course, it is important that you reach out to the right kind of people—those who are trustworthy.

Many other manifestations of pride may repel or threaten to repel others, but I would like to mention just one more: a critical, condemning, judgmental attitude. Sometimes lonely people are lonely because their attitude of superiority renders them hypercritical of others. They rule out developing friendships or even honestly evaluating the potential of friendships with certain

---

36. This, of course, should not be used as an excuse not to love them biblically.

37. The Bible does speak of the importance of having a good reputation (Prov. 22:1; Eccl. 7:1; 1 Tim. 3:7), but it is a sin to idolize your good name. See John 12:43 as well as my book *Pleasing People: How Not to Be an "Approval Junkie"* (Phillipsburg, NJ: P&R Publishing, 2007).

groups of people because they make premature judgments about them based on very flimsy evidence.

Fear. There are probably as many manifestations of fear as there are of pride. But perhaps the two most associated with loneliness are the *fear of being rejected* and the *fear of being alone for the rest of one's life.*

The fear of rejection paralyzes many. It keeps them not only from reaching out to others but also from revealing who they really are to potential friends.[38] This is akin to the fear of embarrassment, but it is really far worse and more far-reaching. It is difficult enough for us to face short-lived embarrassment, but the lingering sting of hurt and rejection, perhaps even betrayal, from someone we trusted is much worse.

Yet, as difficult as that is, we must guard against allowing sinful fear to keep us from reaching out to others in the body of Christ. Fellow believers have been put in our lives for our mutual growth and encouragement. Instead of giving in to such fear, there are times when Christians—after making reasonable assessments of another person's character—may have to apply 1 John 4:18 to their thinking: "'There is no fear in love, but perfect love casts out fear.' If I get hurt or rejected as a result of reaching out to this person, God will give me the grace to handle the hurt; I'm not going to let sinful fear keep me from loving this person or from allowing him or her to love and minister to me as the Bible commands."

The fear of being alone for the rest of your life can be crippling. But that is not the worst of it! The desire for companionship, and commensurate fear of never having it, can be so strong that it tempts many into all manner of sin: sexual immorality, substance abuse, close friendships with dangerous people, and even suicide. While it is true that God doesn't promise everyone

38. Of course, you should take care not to reveal too much to those who have not proven themselves trustworthy and wise, but sinful fear should not keep you from seeking out a "burden bearer" (see Gal. 6:2) who is willing to share in your needs and struggles.

a lifelong companion, it is also true that the Bible encourages every man to consider having his own wife and every woman to consider having her own husband. For the married and the single alike, the local church provides fellowship that can blunt the edge of loneliness, and the Holy Spirit himself can be a constant companion to the believer who feels the intense pain of loneliness. So to prophesy about or imagine the future as one of abject, interminable loneliness without factoring God's grace and help into that future time is to make false prophecies that only intensify feelings of loneliness and may lead to destructive and alienating behaviors. It is to rob yourself of biblical hope and cultivate a mindset of despair.

Selfishness. As I have explained elsewhere,[39] selfishness is the mother of all sins. It is the one sin out of which, in one way or another, all the others flow. Selfishness, more than any other sin, is what keeps us from loving our neighbors. We are so consumed with our own needs and desires that we do not see the needs and desires of those around us.[40]

When we focus on ourselves more than on God, we actually intensify our loneliness in several ways. For one thing, our failure to obey the two greatest commandments cuts off opportunities for us to develop new friendships. Second, sooner or later our selfishness is perceived by others who are offended by it and tempted to withdraw from us. Third, our desire to separate ourselves from others in order to seek our own interests (Prov. 18:1) tempts us to be suspicious of others and their potential agendas and to avoid those who otherwise might offer us their own useful interpretations of what is happening inside and around us.[41]

---

39. See Lou Priolo, *Selfishness: From Loving Yourself to Loving Your Neighbor* (Phillipsburg, NJ: P&R Publishing, 2010).

40. Selfishness often disguises itself as a form of entitlement. Entitlement is noxious and is repulsive to many, while gratitude—the antithesis of entitlement—is attractive to most people.

41. "Whoever trusts in his own mind is a fool, but he who walks in wisdom will be delivered" (Prov. 28:26).

When we self-isolate, we remove ourselves from those who can help to balance our thoughts by correcting our incomplete or erroneous perceptions and patterns of thinking.

Sometimes our selfishness is related to a fear of losing autonomy. The thought that someone else might somehow keep us from doing what we want to do causes us to withdraw from those whom God intends to use to help and encourage us. The inordinate fear of being controlled by others tempts us to inordinately control those things that are not ours to control but rather God's.

Sinful anger. Wayne Mack explains the spiraling connection between loneliness and anger this way: "A lonely person often becomes angry at his situation, and as a result, becomes lonelier. He feels sorry for himself and becomes even lonelier. The downward spiral continues, with anger giving birth to depression, depression to more anger, and all of these to guilt. Guilt often leads to anxiety and soon enough, destruction is knocking at the door as his problems grow and his soul becomes overwhelmed."[42]

God warns Christians to stay away from angry people.

> Do not associate with a man given to anger;
> Or go with a hot-tempered man,
> Or you will learn his ways
> And find a snare for yourself. (Prov. 22:24–25 NASB95)

Of course, before avoiding a fellow believer who struggles with life-dominating anger, typically we should confront and try to restore him or her (Matt. 18:15–18; Luke 17:3; Gal. 6:1). Yet most people understandably shudder at the thought of snuggling up to porcupines.

Contentiousness and irritability. Some men and women, even if they do not struggle with outbursts of anger, fit the biblical category of a contentious person. "Like charcoal to hot embers

42. Mack, *Out of the Blues*, 97.

and wood to fire, so is a contentious man to kindle strife" (Prov. 26:21 NASB).

Have you ever tried to picture this passage? If you put a piece of charcoal next to a couple of embers, it is only a matter of time before a fire will ignite. If you place a piece of dry wood in close proximity to a blazing fire, the wood will burst into flames. If you stay too long in the presence of a contentious person, it is just a matter of time before your conversation will detonate into a quarrel. The point that Solomon is making here is that this person's presence is best avoided. If you are a contentious person, you are driving away the potential friends and helpers who follow Solomon's advice.[43]

The sins I've detailed in this section do not represent a complete taxonomy of self-destructive and off-putting attitudes, although they are among the most common. If you have anyone in your life who knows you well and would be honest and objective enough to help you to see such things, it may be beneficial to ask him or her what else you should consider putting on your list.

Prayerfully ask God to show you if there are other sins that may be contributing to your loneliness.

7. Cultivate thoughts, motives, attitudes, and actions that are conducive to developing biblical friendships.

Not only is it important to understand that the character flaws we possess may repel potential friends, but it is also wise to build into our lives those specific Christlike character traits that enhance our attractiveness and make us more of a blessing to others.

Most people find certain attributes very appealing. The most important one is love.[44] Love is the big umbrella under which all these other attributes take shelter. There is something irresist-

---

43. This paragraph is adapted from Lou Priolo, *Resolving Conflict: How to Make, Disturb, and Keep Peace* (Phillipsburg, NJ: P&R Publishing, 2016), 215.

44. This shouldn't surprise Bible-literate Christians, for we understand that the great commandment is to love (Matt. 22:36–40; 1 Cor. 13; 1 Tim. 1:5).

ible about people who are obvious givers rather than takers. They seemingly could not care less about what others think about them. Instead, they express their desire to meet the needs of those they come into contact with and show no hint of wanting anything in return. Here are a few more qualities that God and *most reasonable people* highly value.

Sincerity. Genuineness and freedom from hypocrisy are qualities most people want to see in their closest friends. We want our friends to be authentic "what you see is what you get" kinds of people (Rom. 12:9; 2 Cor. 1:12; 2:17; Col. 3:22; 1 Peter 1:22; 2:1).

Transparency. Similarly, we want our friends to reveal who they really are to us and not withhold information we need to rightly relate to them as friends. We want them to be truthful with us (2 Cor. 6:11–13; Eph. 4:25).

Humility. People who are not pretentious but acknowledge their own shortcomings and weaknesses are much easier to build friendships with than those who arrogantly pretend to be more than they really are, quickly become defensive, think too highly of themselves, talk much more than they listen, speak boastfully, and are excessively competitive. Sooner or later, friendships with proud people hit the rocks (Prov. 13:10; 18:2; Matt. 6:1–2; Rom. 12:3; 1 Cor. 13:4; 2 Cor. 10:12).

Tolerance. How tolerant are you of those whose speech, behavior, and worldview are different from yours—especially with respect to those things that are not clearly delineated in Scripture? Would others say you are nitpicky, overcritical, sinfully judgmental, or censorious? The ability to be accepting of those who think differently (while not accepting any unbiblical values they may hold) is something that people find attractive. It is also a quality the Bible says Christians should demonstrate toward one another (Rom. 2:1–4; 14:1–12; 15:7; Eph. 4:1–3).

Faith. A sincere faith in God that exudes a Christ-centered self-confidence is another quality most Christians want in their friends. But fearful, anxious, and panicky people can become tedious to others. People want friends who not only trust in the promises of God but also can share that faith and confidence with them in times of trouble.

Joyfulness. There is something about a joy-filled Christian that is spellbindingly attractive. Others are drawn to that person in the hope that some of his or her joy may rub off.[45] It is rare to meet people who are filled with joy, but when you meet them, you don't forget them.

Godly affection. In addition to the five times the Bible commands Christians to greet one another with a holy kiss (Rom. 16:16; 1 Cor. 16:20; 2 Cor. 13:12; 1 Thess. 5:26; 1 Peter 5:14), we read in Romans 12:10, "Love one another with brotherly affection." And there are other biblical examples of showing affection.[46] According to Luke 7:7–10, Jesus didn't need to touch people in order to heal them, but have you noticed how many he touched anyway? Down through the centuries, friends have shown affection to friends. Nonsexual, familial expressions of love between friends—whether they be kisses, hugs, handshakes, hand-holding, or pats on the shoulder or arm—have generally been understood as such.

Some are uncomfortable with such expressions of brotherly love. If you are one of them, perhaps you should prayerfully study what the Bible teaches about such things in the hope of becoming more comfortable with receiving and giving these gestures of love.

45. Check out 2 Corinthians 7:4–14 for an example of the communicable nature of joy.
46. For example, by embracing or touching (1 Sam. 20:41; Mark 1:41; 10:13; Luke 7:38; John 20:17; Acts 20:37; 23:19).

8. Get out of your comfort zone—get up and get out!

What is the point of sitting alone in your room? Life may not be a cabaret, my friend, but company (the right kind of company, at least) often beats hours and days of isolation. And, yes, I know it is sometimes hard to motivate yourself to be with other people. But by God's grace we are called to motivate ourselves. We have to fight thoughts like these:

- "I just don't feel like being around others today."
- "I wouldn't be a fun friend to be around right now."
- "I couldn't bear it if I reached out to someone and was turned down or rejected."
- "I don't want to appear too needy."
- "I don't want to pester people with my problems."
- "It's better to be alone in my room than alone in a social setting."
- "The people in my world (my church, school, or workplace) are wired differently than I am—they just wouldn't understand me."

Don't let these unbiblical thoughts and excuses keep you from receiving love from, and giving it to, those God has placed in your life. And, if you don't recognize what is unbiblical about them, may I suggest that you highlight those thoughts and, in your quiet time this week, open your Bible and analyze them biblically. I have included a worksheet in appendix A to facilitate this process.

Practice serving others. And don't selfishly keep them from the blessings and eternal rewards that are due them as a result of ministering to you. Meditate on this in light of Matthew 10:41–42, Luke 6:38, and Ephesians 6:7–8.

9. Tell someone you trust that you are feeling lonely.

As Christians, we are to bear one another's burdens. Do not let the fear of being perceived as too needy keep you from using all the resources God has provided through his church. Is there an elder, deacon, or Titus 2 kind of man or woman in your fellowship to whom you could reach out? Perhaps someone in your small group, Bible study, or campus ministry might be willing to help. What about Christian organizations that provide helplines or hotlines as well as trained counselors to offer help to those who are struggling with isolation?[47] Let me say it again: please do not selfishly rob someone else of the blessing of ministering to you.

10. Focus on how you can love others rather than on how others aren't loving you.

More and more I find myself giving this counsel to many of the married members of our church: "This week please try to focus more on how you can show love to your spouse than on how your spouse may not be showing love to you." When we focus on how we can meet the needs of others in the present rather than focusing on how others are treating us or might treat us in the future, often our struggles with fear, worry, anxiety, jealousy, and irrational suspicion will quickly subside. This "loving others as you love yourself" principle can also take the edge off loneliness. There are scientific reasons for this, which have to do with the release of endorphins, as well as biblical reasons (Acts 20:35, for example: "It is more blessed to give than to receive").

I concur with Mack's important suggestion: "Studying the 'one-another' passages in Scripture will be very beneficial in helping us to better understand our responsibilities to other believers and the qualities that will produce meaningful relationships. It is my firm conviction, supported by numerous examples of people that I have counseled through severe loneliness, that those who struggle in this way are failing in some aspect of these one-another commands and qualities. And I am equally convinced that lonely

47. For example, the Association of Certified Biblical Counselors (ACBC) and the International Association of Biblical Counselors (IABC) both have trained counselors available for conference-call counseling.

people can develop deep and satisfying friendships when they put these things into practice."[48]

Mack also suggests that lonely individuals identify specific people with whom they will practice these one-another commands, make a list of the specific ways they will practice these passages with each individual, and keep a journal about their attempts to do so. Perhaps this is something you could do as well.

Your motive for obedience in this area—as with every area in the Christian life—is crucially important. If you attempt to love others primarily to assuage your loneliness, God may not bless your efforts—he will likely see them as a self-serving gimmick rather than a true manifestation of love. But if you focus on obeying the second greatest commandment because you desire to please and obey your Lord, you may rightfully claim the promise of James 1:25: "The one who looks into the perfect law, the law of liberty, and perseveres, being no hearer who forgets but a doer who acts, *he will be blessed in his doing.*"[49]

11. Don't compare yourself to others.

I saw a bumper sticker a few years ago that caught my eye. Although it was a bit snarky, it is the stark reality for many. In essence, it said, "I don't need Facebook—I have *real* friends." For all the good that social media provides, there are certain dangers associated with its misuse. In addition to tempting us to waste countless hours and perhaps even become hooked on it, social media invites us to compare ourselves with others who post only those things about themselves that they want others to see.

The source of inferiority is often comparison. The Bible warns us about comparing ourselves with others: "Not that we dare to classify or compare ourselves with some of those who are commending themselves. But when they measure themselves by one another and compare themselves with one another, they

48. Mack, *Out of the Blues*, 106.
49. That is, he will be blessed *in the process of* doing.

are without understanding" (2 Cor. 10:12). You will always find people who fare better or worse than you in one area of their lives or for one moment in time. Comparing yourself to others not only fosters discontent, jealousy, and self-pity but also intensifies feelings of loneliness and isolation.

Comparing ourselves today to where we were yesterday, last month, or last year may have some value in showing how we have grown and developed. But Jesus Christ is the ultimate reference point. And I'm not just talking about his godly character—although becoming more and more like him is our constant pursuit and should be our most important point of comparison. I'm talking about the way he lived during his time on earth. Did Jesus drive a brand-new car or live in an elegant house? Did he wear expensive designer jeans and sneakers? Did he vacation at Lake Tahoe or in the Italian Alps and post gorgeous shots of himself in those locations on Instagram? Come to think of it, did Jesus comb through dozens of photos to find the most flattering shot of himself, then spend twenty minutes digitally enhancing the image before posting it for all the world to see? Did he spend hundreds of dollars on glamor shots so that those who surfed his page would be tempted to compare themselves with him? Did all his friends, followers, and family adore him at all times?

The problem isn't just social media. After all, there was no internet when Paul warned the Corinthians about the foolishness of making uninformed comparisons. We mingle with people every day at work, school, church functions, and social gatherings. The temptation to compare ourselves to those with whom we interact—perhaps even to compete with them—is all around us.

One of the most helpful bits of advice I can offer, as a counselor, to those who struggle with covetousness, jealousy, envy, or any other destructive by-product of comparison is to practice implementing Romans 12:15: "*Rejoice with those who rejoice*, weep with those who weep." When I was single and very desirous of being married, I would truly be happy for my friends who were married or engaged. I would thank the Lord for his goodness in giving them people with whom they could share their lives. I would pray for their happiness. Then I would remind the Lord of my desire for a wife and ask him to grant that desire, if it were his will, in his time. By faith I would anticipate his goodness to me in the future. I wouldn't allow myself to become envious because God had given someone else what he had not yet given me.

12. Get to know your Best Friend.

If you are a follower of Christ and have put your trust solely in his redemptive work on the cross, your best friend is the Holy Spirit, who lives inside you.

The Holy Spirit is your constant companion. He is the source of your power and your personal relationship to Jesus Christ. He is there to comfort, empower, illumine, sanctify, and intercede for you in your loneliness. You need him, and you have him. He is present to enable you to live a life pleasing to God and to facilitate your relationship with him.

American Express says, "Don't leave home without it." As a Christian, you don't leave home without the Holy Spirit. Everywhere you go, you take him with you. You may not always realize it, but he is inside you. Capital One asks, "What's in your wallet?" Perhaps you've got some credit cards in your wallet, but if you are a Christian, you carry around in your person another person.

There is no other person quite like him. "The Holy Spirit is a person. He is not a mystical force or metaphysical influence. He is a divine person—the third person of the Trinity—and acknowledging that fact is absolutely essential to an orthodox understanding of who He is. Personhood has personality traits, and personality includes intellect, emotions, and will. And these attributes are characteristic of the Holy Spirit."[50]

50. John MacArthur, *The Silent Shepherd: The Care, Comfort, and Correction of the Holy Spirit*, 2nd ed. (Colorado Springs: David C Cook, 2012), 5.

Since the Spirit is a person, having a right relationship with him is the key to your living life in a manner that is both pleasing to God and satisfying to you. If you have been born again, he indwells you for sure, but whether he fills you at any given point is largely up to you. Moreover, he can be grieved if you allow unconfessed sin to linger in your life. Such sin interferes with your fellowship with God and increases your sense of loneliness and isolation.

When was the last time you said or did something foolish that negatively affected someone you loved very much—someone with whom you were in regular communication? I imagine it was rather distracting, even upsetting. Your ability to focus on other things was diminished because you knew that this relationship had been disturbed by your stupidity. You missed the close fellowship you once had with that loved one. You probably knew that all you had to do to put things right was to humble yourself, repent, and ask forgiveness. When you did and the relationship was restored, you were relieved and able to go about your business without distraction or distress.

Sometimes people are lonely because they *know* that they have offended their best friend and that he simply wants them to acknowledge that they have sinned against him and to commit to depend on him when they are tempted to sin in the future.

We must also guard against quenching the Spirit.[51] So many lonely Christians I have counseled refuse to spend sufficient time in God's Word. In so doing, they in effect quench the Spirit's work in their lives. The Spirit works through the Word.

This leads to the matter of being filled with the Spirit, as Paul commands in Ephesians 5:18. In the Greek, Paul says, "Be ye being filled," meaning that the Christian is to be filled with the Spirit *continuously*. How is that accomplished? Basically, it is a matter of letting the Word of Christ dwell in you (Col. 3:16). This means internalizing and meditating on the Scriptures.

---

51. That is, dismissing or despising his prophetic utterance as unimportant (1 Thess. 5:19–20).

Compare Ephesians 5:18–20 with Colossians 3:16, and you will see that what flows from one also flows from the other.[52] The more the Word of God actively fills your thoughts, the more the Spirit controls your life.

13. Pray.

We speak to God in prayer. He speaks to us in the Word. If the Holy Spirit is indeed your best friend, shouldn't you talk to him often? Shouldn't you regularly pour out your heart before him (Ps. 62:8)? I have counseled more people than I can recall who are lonely yet refuse to pray simply because they are angry (bitter, really) at God. Some of them engage in a sort of super-stition that says, "I have prayed before—to no avail. I'm afraid that if I pray to God, he will continue to disregard my prayer because I'm under some kind of curse. Maybe God is punishing me for something, but I'm not sure what it is." They view God more as their Judge than as their loving heavenly Father. For them, God has become a god other than the God of the Bible. Their bad theology is exacerbating their problem.

Those who struggle with this superstition remain prayerless because prayer doesn't give them the immediate relief they are looking for—relief they then seek in other places. Prayer is hard work.[53] Lazy people don't want to do it. Marriage takes work, friendships take work, and walking with God takes work too.

Enoch *walked* with God, and he was not, for God took him. (Gen. 5:24)

If we live by the Spirit, let us also *walk* by the Spirit. (Gal. 5:25 NASB95)

---

52. I have written about this and explained it in more detail elsewhere (as have others). See Lou Priolo, "Honey, You Need a Bath," chap. 9 of *The Complete Husband: A Practical Guide for Improved Biblical Husbanding*, rev. and expanded ed. (Phillipsburg, NJ: P&R Publishing, 2017).

53. "Epaphras, who is one of you and a servant of Christ Jesus, sends greetings. He is always wrestling [agonizing, *agonizomai* in Greek] in prayer for you" (Col. 4:12 NIV).

I therefore, a prisoner for the Lord, urge you to *walk* in a manner worthy of the calling to which you have been called. (Eph. 4:1)

For at one time you were darkness, but now you are light in the Lord. *Walk* as children of light. (Eph. 5:8)

We exhorted each one of you and encouraged you and charged you to *walk* in a manner worthy of God, who calls you into his own kingdom and glory. (1 Thess. 2:12)

Are you putting as much time, effort, and thought into your walk with God (in general) and your prayer life (in particular) as you should? Could it be that your loneliness is one of those smoke detectors we saw earlier that is indicating that God wants you to more highly prioritize conversing with him?

14. Don't lose perspective!

A little loneliness is more tolerable than you may realize. Be careful to guard your heart from magnifying a *tolerable* trial into an *unbearable* one. You will have to live with some amount of loneliness as long as you are "absent from the Lord" (2 Cor. 5:6 NASB).

Living in a sin-cursed world precludes ultimate happiness in this life. We live not for this world but for the next. Until the Lord returns, sin, suffering, sickness, and Satan will be with us. Loneliness can be a good thing not only because it lets us know that it's time to draw closer to God but also because it makes us long to be with Christ for all eternity.

15. Keep track of your loneliness.

As a counselor, I know that there are benefits to keeping certain kinds of journals. They not only help us to understand more clearly the nature of our struggles but also often reveal certain patterns in our thinking. Additionally, journaling may reveal information about the times and even the circumstances in which we are most likely to struggle. You might find it beneficial to keep a journal of your loneliness that includes the date, time, circumstances, and perhaps even the things you say to yourself during those times. Finding a pastor or trained biblical counselor to review and unpack your journal may be more beneficial than you might expect. In appendix B, I have included a sample of what such a journal might look like.

16. Get a medical checkup.

If you have been suffering from depression that you believe is related to loneliness or isolation, you may want to consider having a physician run some tests on your blood. There may be organic factors at play that are medically treatable, such as a problematic thyroid or a thyroid disease, sleep deprivation or apnea, dieting issues, vitamin or mineral deficiencies, side effects from the use of certain substances, or other chronic diseases or conditions.

17. Consider (meditate on) the solitude of Christ.

Jesus had no spouse or biological children and no place to lay his head. He had fickle friends who forsook him in his greatest moment of need and multitudes of people who wanted him dead. Yet he knew that the Father was with him. For various reasons, he would occasionally spend time alone (Matt. 14:13; Mark 1:35–37; Luke 4:1–2, 14–15; 5:15–16; 6:12–13; 22:39–44). How much happier do you suppose you would be if you thought in terms of the benefits of solitude—such as an opportunity to spend time with God in prayer—rather than the miseries of loneliness?

18. Practice thankfulness.

Providentially, while I have been writing this section of the booklet, my daily Bible readings have taken me through the Psalms. I was especially struck by these verses:

51

Hear, O my people, and I will speak;
    O Israel, I will testify against you.
    I am God, your God.
Not for your sacrifices do I rebuke you;
    your burnt offerings are continually before me.
I will not accept a bull from your house
    or goats from your folds.
For every beast of the forest is mine,
    the cattle on a thousand hills.
I know all the birds of the hills,
    and all that moves in the field is mine.

If I were hungry, I would not tell you,
    for the world and its fullness are mine.
Do I eat the flesh of bulls
    or drink the blood of goats?
Offer to God a sacrifice of thanksgiving,
    and perform your vows to the Most High,
and call upon me in the day of trouble;
    I will deliver you, and you shall glorify me. (Ps. 50:7–15)

I have recently been convicted not only of excessive grumbling and complaining but also of not being grateful to the Lord for all he has done for me and for who he is. Since I haven't had to offer any animal sacrifices lately, I really hadn't set apart a specific time to offer praise to God other than Sunday worship. When I realized that, I realized how truly ungrateful I've been. Do you ever make sacrifices of thanksgiving to God—not by killing animals but rather setting apart time to give him praise?

And, by the way, this is not just an Old Testament expression. Hebrews 13:15 says, "Through him then let us continually offer up a sacrifice of praise to God, that is, the fruit of lips that acknowledge his name."

19. Learn how to be content in your current state of solitude.

At the heart of learning to deal with loneliness is learning to be content. Meditate on these characteristics of contentment:[54]

- Contentment is realizing that God has already provided everything that I (as a Christian) need to glorify and enjoy him (Phil. 4:11–13).
- Contentment is realizing that true satisfaction can come only from building my life around those things that cannot be taken away or destroyed (Matt. 6:19–20).
- Contentment is delighting in God more than in anything else (Ps. 37:4).
- Contentment is being able to adjust the level of my desires to the condition and purpose chosen for me by God (Phil. 4:11–12).
- Contentment is willingly submitting to and delighting in God's wise and loving disposal (his divine distribution) in every condition of life (Job 1:20–22).
- Contentment is knowing how to use the things of this world without becoming engrossed in them (1 Cor. 7:29–31).
- Contentment is thanking God even in circumstances in which I used to murmur and complain (Phil. 2:14; 1 Thess. 5:18).

Here is the bottom line: as a Christian, you must learn to accept the fact that God has placed you in your current condition for his purposes and for your ultimate good. Although you may prayerfully look for lawful ways to ameliorate your condition, you should not allow yourself to respond sinfully in your heart or with your words, attitudes, and actions. You can do all things through Christ who strengthens you.

54. For a more detailed discussion of these points, see Lou Priolo, *Discontentment: Why Am I So Unhappy?* (Phillipsburg, NJ: P&R Publishing, 2012), 10–28. This little book contains very helpful information that may further strengthen your ability to deal with loneliness.

I trust that at least some of what I have written here has not only helped you to understand the various causes of loneliness and factors that exacerbate it but also offered you real help and hope from the gospel of Christ. This booklet (like its author) is very dense. It will probably require more than one reading. And it will require more than simply reading. Some of the remedies I have prescribed will have to be worked out over time. It is not just a matter of taking a few "spiritual pills" to ease the pain but rather a matter of getting an infusion every week, of having to change your diet, and of going through the rigors of physical therapy. But God promises his children help! Not the eradication of all loneliness in this life but the grace—the supernatural ability—to handle your loneliness in a way that glorifies God and minimizes your misery. May God be with you in your trial as you apply what you have learned.

APPENDIX A

Reconstructed Thoughts Worksheet

WHEN WE experience loneliness, our thoughts can be our worst enemies. But they can also serve to deliver us from despair and offer us biblical help and hope. Because we can speak to ourselves with incredible speed, because our thoughts are so intertwined with our desires, and because we have learned to listen to ourselves rather than talk to ourselves, it can be difficult for us to detect unbiblical thinking. Thought patterns of self-pity, discontent, anxiety, and ingratitude often run through our minds as quickly as polluted water through a sieve. We may even attribute to God qualities that are inconsistent with his character. In the Holy Scriptures, God has given us both a filter to catch and strain out impurities and a chemical purifier to repair the molecular makeup of the water flow.

Use the space in column 1 of the chart that follows to record the sinful thought patterns that you find yourself regularly rehearsing in your mind. Then go to your Bible to find those passages that might address each of those sinful thought patterns and record them in column 2. In column 3, evaluate and critique each unbiblical thought in light of those Scripture passages, recording what the Bible says is correct, or incorrect, about what you have told yourself. Finally, in column 4, restructure your thoughts so that they are biblically accurate and reflect gospel hope and help. When you catch yourself musing over or muttering those unbiblical thoughts, try to recall the corrected thoughts you have written out—or, better still, memorize them verbatim in advance—so that you can replace them on the spot. Start talking to yourself rather than listening to yourself!

My Thought	Scripture References	Reason This Thought Is Unbiblical	Biblically Adjusted Thought
I wouldn't be a fun friend to be around today.	Proverbs 17:17; 27:17 Ecclesiastes 4:9–10 Philippians 2:1–11 Colossians 3:13 1 Thessalonians 5:11	Being a friend is the biblical requirement. The fun part is optional. I should be more concerned about how I can love others and meet their needs and be willing to let them meet my needs than I am about being or having "fun."	It is more important that I minister to my friends and allow them to minister to me than it is for me to be perceived as a fun friend. Besides, if we conduct our time together as the Bible says friends should, it will probably be more enjoyable than if I selfishly isolate myself.
It's better to be alone and miserable in my room than alone and awkward in a social setting.	Psalm 23:4; 27:1 Proverbs 18:1 Matthew 22:36–40 2 Timothy 1:7 1 Peter 3:13–17 1 John 4:18	I should be less focused on pleasing myself and more focused on pleasing God. I should be more concerned about loving God and neighbor than I am about my feelings. Even if the feelings of being in a social setting are unpleasant, ultimately the feelings of guilt for making a selfish choice may be worse. And if I go where God wants me to go and I have unpleasant feelings, in a sense I will be suffering for righteousness's sake, which is better than suffering for my sin.	It's not a sin to feel awkward. God will give me the grace to face my fear, especially if I go to this event because I am trying to please him. If I give in to my feelings and continue this pattern of isolating myself, I will be persisting in selfish and fearful decision-making that is ultimately going to make me more miserable.

My Thought	Scripture References	Reason This Thought Is Unbiblical	Biblically Adjusted Thought

My Thought	Scripture References	Reason This Thought Is Unbiblical	Biblically Adjusted Thought

APPENDIX B

Loneliness Journal

After filling out this worksheet, go over it with a church leader or biblical counselor to see if he or she may be able to help you process and interpret your lonely experience through a more biblical lens.

Date: _____   Time of Day: _____ AM / PM

What were the circumstances that prompted my loneliness?

_____
_____
_____
_____
_____

What did I say to myself during my bout with loneliness?

_____
_____
_____
_____
_____

What would have been a more biblical way to process the loneliness I was experiencing?

_____
_____
_____
_____
_____

Also from P&R Publishing

Honest self-assessment is hard. Even Christians trust their hearts more than they should. And when the heart is filled with rage ("I will have my own way"), sensuality ("I will gratify myself regardless of the sin involved"), or pride ("I deserve whatever my heart desires"), indulging its desires all too easily leads to acts that were previously unimaginable.

This book is an excellent resource for all who want to understand how the passions and motivations of their hearts can lead them into sins of any kind. Using this resource, sinful passions can be identified and resisted—and, by the grace of God, they can be forgiven in Christ.

"The unfolding of the truth about the heart is for any malady of the soul. This book can instruct the reader to develop good devotional and Bible-reading habits to overcome the temptations of sin in all areas of life. This book contains so many jewels for understanding the heart that reading it [is] like searching for gold."
—**Bill Shannon**, Pastor of Discipleship Counseling, Grace Community Church, Sun Valley, California

Also from P&R Publishing

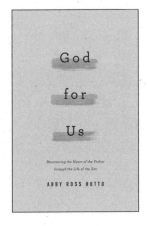

Does God feel far off and unconcerned—or even against you? Abby Hutto presents thirteen stories about Jesus from John's gospel that dispel our distrust and confusion by narrating through Jesus who God truly is. She interweaves testimonials from modern-day believers with further Scripture and discussion questions to assure us that God is for us and longs to draw our confused, distrusting hearts to himself.

"A unique book that will comfort, challenge, and compel you."
—Ellen Mary Dykas

"It's refreshing to come across a book that is not only theologically sound but also emotionally compelling. . . . We discover a Savior who is for us as well as with us, and a love and grace that is there to be received by every kind of person."
—Scott Sauls

Also from P&R Publishing

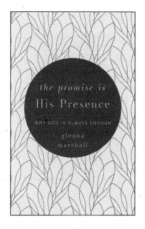

God's presence among his people set him apart from ancient pagan gods. His presence on earth as God Incarnate split history in two. And today his presence is one of the most significant means of his goodness to us. Interweaving her story of faith and doubt amid suffering, Glenna traces the theme of God's presence from Genesis to Revelation and shows what it means for us in our own daily joys and struggles.

"I was convicted in the sweetest way to remember that abiding in the Lord's presence through his Word is enough for me in the midst of my every fear, unmet desire, struggle, and joy."
—**Kristie Anyabwile**

"If you are weary, discouraged, or suffering, you will find refreshment, encouragement, and comfort in these pages."
—**Marissa Henley**

Was this booklet helpful to you?
Consider writing a review online.
The author appreciates your feedback!

Or write to P&R at editorial@prpbooks.com
with your comments. We'd love to hear from you.